The Maple Tree

by Kathleen Cox
illustrated by Pamela Anzalotti

Editorial Offices: Glenview, Illinois • Parsippany, New Jersey • New York, New York
Sales Offices: Needham, Massachusetts • Duluth, Georgia • Glenview, Illinois
Coppell, Texas • Ontario, California • Mesa, Arizona

Every effort has been made to secure permission and provide appropriate credit for photographic material. The publisher deeply regrets any omission and pledges to correct errors called to its attention in subsequent editions.

Unless otherwise acknowledged, all photographs are the property of Scott Foresman, a division of Pearson Education.

Photo locators denoted as follows: Top (T), Center (C), Bottom (B), Left (L), Right (R), Background (Bkgd)

Illustrations by Pamela Anzalotti

7 Farrell Grehan/Corbis; 14 Corbis; 16 (CL, BR) Richard Fukuhara/Corbis, (B) Clive; Boursnell/DK Images; 19 DK Images

ISBN: 0-328-13443-0

7 8 9 10 V0G1 14 13 12 11 10 09 08

It is the middle of February in rural Vermont. Sugar maples cover a snowy mountainside. A river flows along the base of the mountain. A group of about 250 sugar maple trees grows on flat land on the other side of the river.

The trees are in a sugar bush, or maple orchard. A farmer owns the sugar bush and lives there with his family in an old white farmhouse. Maple sugaring is a modern industry in which goods are made to be sold, but this farmer uses a traditional method of making sweet maple syrup.

In winter there are no leaves on the sugar maples. They are completely bare. The few pine trees on the farmer's land are the only trees that are green this time of year.

The maple trees in the farmer's sugar bush are at least one hundred years old. Each tree is about eighty-five feet tall, and each trunk is about five feet around. Their trunks are so wide that it is almost impossible to stretch your arms around them!

At this time in mid-February, the farmer knows that he must pay attention to the temperature. The season is slowly shifting from winter to spring. Sitting in an easy chair in his **parlor,** the farmer glances up from his newspaper and looks out the window. The outside of the glass pane is **etched** with **frost.** He knows the temperature will drop below freezing at night.

The next day, he walks along the snowy path to his sugar bush. He sees that the frost, which collected overnight, has melted on rocks by the side of the river. The days are getting warmer. The daytime temperature is above freezing.

This pattern of temperatures above freezing by day and below freezing by night tells the farmer that something is happening inside his sugar maples. A frozen mixture of sugar and minerals has been stored all winter under the tree bark. Now it has thawed.

The farmer knows that this mixture is turning into a watery sap that will pump through a natural pipeline that exists inside the roots, the tree trunk, and all the branches. This sap is food and energy for the tree.

All maple trees make sap. Sugar maples and black maples make an especially sweet sap. This sap can be tapped, or collected, and turned into maple sugar and maple syrup. We pour sweet maple syrup over steamy, hot pancakes. We make this syrup into tasty maple candy and maple sugar cookies.

During the next five weeks, while the season hovers between winter and spring, the farmer will be very busy. This is the sugaring season. His work day starts early in the morning and lasts until late at night.

This farmer is tapping trees.

The farmer has already checked the condition of the taps, or spouts, that he drilled into each tree trunk. Most of his trees are so big that they have several taps drilled into different sides of their trunks.

Now the farmer hangs a metal bucket from each tap. These taps connect to the sugar maple's pumping system and allow the sap to drain into the buckets. Every day the farmer empties the sap from the buckets on his trees. He takes the heavy pails of sap to his sugarhouse.

The farmer props open the door to his sugarhouse so that a cool **draft** comes inside. A large wood-burning stove heats up the sugarhouse as he pours all the sap into a large rectangular pan that is set on top of a stove. This shallow metal pan is called an evaporator.

As the fire heats the evaporator, the sap begins to bubble. Then the sap comes to a boil. About six hours later, the sap, which was very watery, has become a thick maple syrup.

Every year the farmer and his family celebrate their first batch of maple syrup. His children put a scoop of packed snow into a separate dish for each of them. They pour hot maple syrup over the snow. It turns into a chewy taffy.

Neighbors often come to visit the farmer while he works in his sugarhouse. They are **fascinated** by the big pans of bubbling sap. But they are surprised to hear that it takes about sixty gallons of sap to produce just one gallon of the best quality maple syrup.

Young children also come to the sugar bush during the sugaring season. The farmer always asks them if they would like to carry a bucket of sap to the sugarhouse. Most of the visiting children are **timid.** They quickly say no. A look of near **terror** covers their faces as they imagine spilling the valuable sap as they carry it from a tree to the sugarhouse.

The farmer uses an evaporator to boil sap.

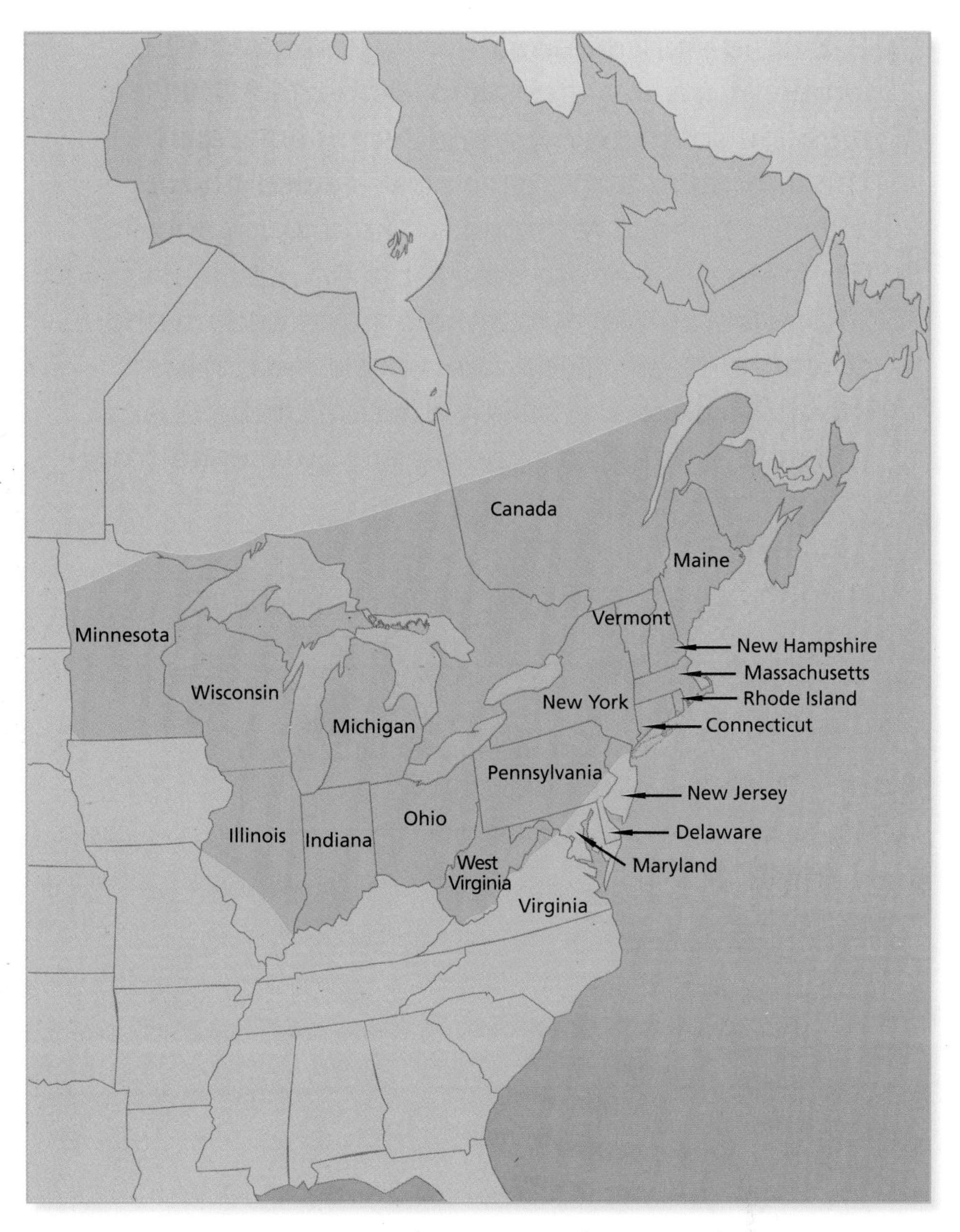

Sugaring maples grow in these North American areas for commercial maple sugar production.

By mid-April the weather has changed. The temperature at night is above freezing. The sugaring season is over, and spring has set in. The migrating birds, which traveled south for the winter, have returned to the sugar maple trees. These trees are now budding new leaves. Squirrels scamper across the ground and up and down the trees. Wildflowers push their new shoots through the soil by the side of the river. The maple trees have completely awakened from their winter sleep.

The roots of the sugar maple reach out far.

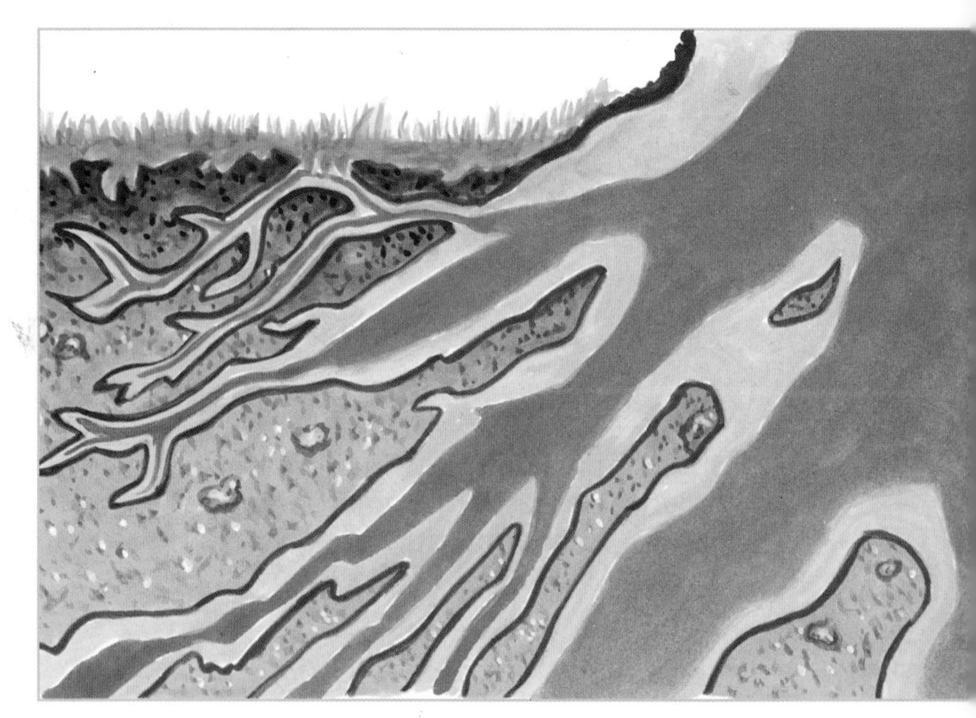

All the maple trees that grow in the northeastern United States and parts of Canada have shaken off their slumber. During the next few months, they put all their energy into growing. Maple trees can live for hundreds of years. During their first hundred years of existence, they grow about a foot each year.

The maple tree's roots anchor the tree to the ground. They burrow deep in the soil and push out in every direction. The huge network of roots has spread like an enormous open hand with dozens and dozens of outstretched fingers in the ground. The deep roots help keep the tree from toppling over during strong winds. The roots also gather the nutrients the tree needs to make sap.

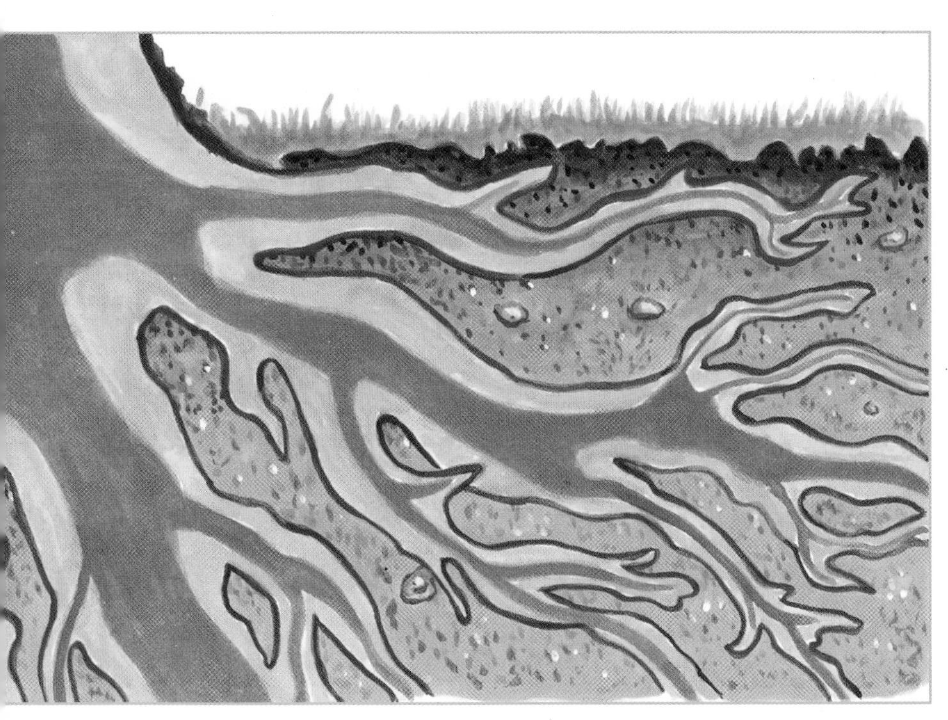

The tiny buds on the sugar maple branches turn into full-sized green leaves by the end of spring. Bees pollinate some of the little flowers that appear on the twigs of the maple.

All day long the leaves draw in a gas called carbon dioxide from the air. All day long chlorophyll, which creates the green color of each leaf, draws in energy from the Sun.

This is a maple tree in spring.

The chlorophyll uses the Sun's energy to mix carbon dioxide with water coming up from the roots. This mixture is changed into sugar and becomes more food for the tree. This process, called photosynthesis, releases oxygen into the air for us to breathe.

By the middle of summer, the flowers that were pollinated by the bees turn into fruit. The maple fruit is a winged seed. You may have picked up these seeds and let them spin to the ground like helicopters. Some of the seeds become food for birds, chipmunks, and squirrels. Some of the seeds sprout in the ground and turn into new maple trees. Some of these tiny trees become tasty food for deer.

Soon it is fall. Summer's heat is gone. The days are shorter. The nights are colder and much longer. By now, a corky layer is slowly growing at the base of each stem that connects each leaf to the branch. This corky growth stops water and sap from flowing to the leaf. The leaf's green coloring fades away.

Once the chlorophyll has disappeared, the leaves show off the bright red and orange colors that were hidden under the green in the spring and the summer. This display of color lasts only a few weeks in the fall. Soon the layers of growth on each stem have completely stopped the flow of moisture to each leaf.

The leaves dry out and fall from the maple tree. A gentle breeze or a squirrel scampering across a branch will cause many leaves to fall to the ground. In a few weeks, the leaves will be gone. All the branches on the maple trees will be bare.

This is a maple tree in fall.

In early November, the farmer rakes up the fallen maple leaves in his sugar bush. He knows how much his children love to jump into the pile of faded, crisp leaves.

The farmer also removes tiny new trees that could get in the way of his older sugar maples. He doesn't want new growth to disturb his valuable trees. Finally, he cuts back unwanted branches and chops them into logs that he will use in his fireplace during the winter.

The farmer will use these maple logs to heat his home.

By the end of November, the temperature outside the farmer's house drops to below freezing in the evening. When the farmer and his family go to bed at night, they are grateful for the warmth of their heavy blankets. They are also grateful for the maple logs, which they burn in the fireplace on cold winter nights.

The maple trees all over the United States and Canada take care of themselves during the winter. Their outside skin of bark protects the important pipeline that runs through the trees. The sap that flowed through the branches, trunk, and root system has hardened and turned into starch, which will be stored until the next sugaring season.

When it is time to tap the trees again, the farmer will be ready. He will tap his sugar maples and boil down the sap. He will make the sweet maple syrup for his friends and family to enjoy.

This is a maple tree in winter.

Glossary

draft *n.* a current of air.

etched *v.* engraved a drawing or design.

fascinated *v.* interested greatly; attracted very strongly; charmed.

frost *n.* a freezing condition; temperature below the point at which water freezes.

parlor *n.* a sitting room.

terror *n.* great fear.

timid *adj.* easily frightened; shy.